Cataraqui United Church Cemetery 5

The Grave Whisperer

Angeline Gallant

Published by Angeline Gallant, 2022.

While every precaution has been taken in the preparation of this book, the publisher assumes no responsibility for errors or omissions, or for damages resulting from the use of the information contained herein.

CATARAQUI UNITED CHURCH CEMETERY 5

First edition. November 11, 2022.

Copyright © 2022 Angeline Gallant.

ISBN: 979-8215011447

Written by Angeline Gallant.

Also by Angeline Gallant

Calling Her Heart
Whisper of the Heart
No Turning Back
Forsake Me Not
Hear My Cry
Calling Her Heart Boxed Set Volumes 1-4

FORGET ME NOT
Victoria, Ontario's Babies 1894 - 1895

Keeper Of Secrets
A Lady's Secret

Midnight's Awakening
Heart of the Storm
Walking Through The Storm
Midnight's Awakening boxed set volumes 1-3

Secrets of the Underworld
Deklan's Dragons
Secrets of the Underworld Volumes 1 & 2

Tell My Story Collection
Tell My Story: England 1852

The Grave Whisperer
Wedding Bells in Kingston, Ontario, Canada 1923
St. Paul's Anglican Churchyard Kingston, Ontario, Canada A-B
St. Paul's Anglican Churchyard, Kingston, Ontario, Canada C - D
St. Paul's Anglican Churchyard, Kingston, Ontario, Canada G - H
St. Paul's Anglican Churchyard, Kingston, Ontario, Canada J - N
St. Paul's Anglican Churchyard, Kingston, Ontario, Canada O - R
St. Paul's Anglican Churchyard, Kingston, Ontario, Canada S - T
St. Paul's Anglican Churchyard, Kingston, Ontario T - Z
Small Graveyards & Burial Grounds: Kingston, Ontario, Canada
Cataraqui United Church Cemetery 1
Cataraqui United Church Cemetery 2
Cataraqui United Church Cemetary 3
Cataraqui United Church Cemetery 4
Cataraqui United Church Cemetery 5

The Wolf Whisperer Series
The Cry of the Wolf
Captured Heart

Journey of the Heart
Fate's Legacy
Wolf Whisperer volumes 1 & 2
Endless White
The Wolf Whisperer Volumes 1-4

Standalone
Winds of Change vol 1-3

Watch for more at https://www.goodreads.com/author/show/
19703964.Angeline_Gallant.

Table of Contents

ALBERT EDWARD GIBSON[1]

Albert was born in Canada on January 5, 1861.

He was five years old when Ontario was founded on July 1, 1867.

Albert was 24 years old when he married Ann Jane in Loughborough, Ontario on April 16, 1885.

He was 26 years old when his sister, Rhoda Ann, passed away in 1887.

Albert was 28 years old when his son, Erie Potter, was born in 1889.

He was 35 years old when his father passed away in 1896.

Albert was 42 years old when his mother passed away in 1903.

He was 52 years old when his brother, William Henry, passed away in 1913.

Albert was 66 years old when his sister, Ellen, passed away in 1927.

He was 69 years old when his brother, John Calvin Cummings, passed away on May 29, 1930. His sister, Mary Elizabeth, passed away on October 13th.

Albert was 83 years old when he passed away on December 8, 1944 in San Jose, California. He is buried in the family plot in Kingston, Ontario.

ANNE JANE "ANNIE" (McRORY) GIBSON[2]

Annie was born in 1863.

She was two years old when Ontario was founded on July 1, 1867.

Annie was 19 years old when her brother, George, passed away in 1883.

She was 21 years old when she married Albert Edward in Loughborough, Ontario on April 16, 1885.

Annie was 25 years old when her son, Erie Potter, was born in 1889.

She was 29 years old when her father passed away in 1893.

Annie was 53 years old when her mother passed away in 1917.

She was 69 years old when her brother, Wilson, passed away in 1933.

Annie was 71 years old when her sister, Mary Emma, passed away in 1935.

She was 80 years old when her husband passed away in 1944.

Annie was 83 years old when her brother, William Wallace, passed away in 1947.

She was 85 years old when she passed away in Santa Clara, California in 1949.

EMILY (BENNINGTON) GIBSON[3]

Emily was born in May 1859.

She was seven years old when Ontario was founded on July 1, 1867.

Emily was 11 years old when her mother passed away in 1870.

She was 15 years old when her brother, Thomas, passed away in 1874.

Emily was 19 years old when she married John Calvin Cummings Gibson in Kingston, Ontario on December 25, 1878.

She was 20 years old when her daughter, Ethel Blanch, was born in 1880.

Emily was 21 years old when her son, Robert Bruce, was born in 1881.

She was 23 years old when the mining boom in northern Ontario began in 1883.

Emily was 24 years old when her daughter, Annie Mildred, was born in 1883.

She was 26 years old when her son, Milton, was born in 1886.

Emily was 28 years old when her father passed away in 1888.

She was 37 years old when her brother, George, passed away in 1896.

Emily was 46 years old when Ontario Hydro was established in 1906.

She was 71 years old when her husband passed away in 1930.

Emily was 74 years old when she passed away in 1934. She was Methodist.

JOHN CALVIN CUMMINGS GIBSON[4]

John was born on December 4, 1851.

He was 15 years old when Ontario was founded on July 1, 1867.

John was 19 years old when British Columbia joined the confederation in 1871.

He was 27 years old when he married in Kingston, Ontario on December 25, 1878.

John was 28 years old when he daughter, Ethel Blanch, was born in 1880.

He was 29 years old when his son, Robert Bruce, was born in 1881.

John was 31 years old when his daughter, Annie Mildred, was born in 1883.

He was 34 years old when his son, Milton, was born in 1886.

John was 35 years old when his sister, Rhoda Anne, passed away in 1887.

He was 44 years old when his father passed away in 1896.

John was 51 years old when his mother passed away in 1903.

He was 54 years old when Ontario Hydro was established in 1906.

John was 61 years old when his brother, William Henry, passed away in 1913.

He was 76 years old when his sister, Ellen, passed away in 1927.

John was 78 years old when he passed away in Cataraqui, Ontario on May 29, 1930. He is buried in Kingston.

JOHN EDWARD GIBSON[5]

John was born in 1893.

He was 13 years old when Ontario Hydro was founded in 1906.

John was 29 years old when he married Vera in 1922.

He was 69 years old when his wife passed away in 1962.

John was 74 years old when he passed away in 1967.

MYRTLE ELIZABETH (GUESS) GIBSON[6]

Myrtle was born in Kingston, Ontario on November 9, 1884. She was 21 years old when Ontario Hydro was established in 1906.

Myrtle was 25 years old when she married Robert Bruce in Kingston on June 15, 1910.

She was 26 years old when her mother passed away in 1911. Her son, Robert John, was born that year.

Myrtle was 49 years old when the Dionne Quintuplets were born in 1934.

She was 55 years old when her father passed away in 1940.

Myrtle was 73 years old when her sister, Mary, passed away in 1958.

She was 86 years old when she passed away in 1971.

ROBERT BRUCE GIBSON[7]

Robert was born in Kingston, Ontario on September 1, 1881.

He was 24 years old when Ontario Hydro was established in 1906.

Robert was 28 years old when he married Myrtle Elizabeth in Kingston, Ontario on June 15, 1910.

He was 29 years old when his son, Robert John, was born in 1911.

Robert was 48 years old when his father passed away in 1930.

He was 52 years old when his mother passed away in 1934.

Robert was 80 years old when he passed away in 1962.

ROBERT JOHN "JACK" GIBSON[8]

Jack was born on October 2, 1911 in Kingston, Ontario.

He was 22 years old when the Dionne Quintuplets were born in 1934.

Jack was 50 years old when his father passed away in 1962.

He was 59 years old when his mother passed away in 1971.

Jack was 70 years old when the Canada Act was passed in 1982.

He was 78 years old when he passed away in 1989.

RICHARD GEORGE GIBSON[9]

Richard was born and passed away on April 24, 1955.

VERA MAY (WARTMAN) GIBSON[10]

Vera was born in Kingston on October 1, 1902.

She was three years old when Ontario Hydro was established in 1906.

Vera was 14 years old when her brother, Harold, passed away in 1917.

She was 16 years old when her sister, Edna Pearl, passed away in 1918.

Vera was 19 years old when she married John Edward in Kingston on September 5, 1922.

She was 31 years old when the Dionne Quintuplets were born in 1934.

Vera was 53 years old when her father passed away in 1956.

She was 54 years old when her mother passed away in 1957.

Vera was 59 years old when she passed away in 1962.

WILLIAM EDWARD GILLESPIE[11]

William was born in Ottawa, Ontario on April 26, 1902.

He was three years old when Ontario Hydro was established in 1906.

William was five years old when his brother, Stuart Cummings, passed away in 1907. Stuart was only 11 days old.

He was 31 years old when the Dionne Quintuplets were born in 1934.

William was 41 years old when his brother, Charles Edward Kent, passed away in 1944.

He was 44 years old when he passed away on May 5, 1946.

WILLIAM R. GLOVER[12]

William was born in 1875.

He was eight years old when the mining boom in northern Ontario began in 1883.

William was 88 years old when he passed away in 1963.

MARY ANN (VanLUVEN) GOODELL[13]

Mary was born in 1862. She was Scottish.

She was four years old when Ontario was founded on July 1, 1867.

Mary was eight years old when British Columbia joined the confederation in 1871.

She was 20 years old when she married George in Kingston, Ontario on January 1, 1883.

Mary was 35 years old when her daughter, Pearl, was born in 1898.

She was 40 years old when her daughter, Pearl, passed away in 1903. Pearl was five years old.

Mary was 53 years old when her mother passed away in 1916.

She was 71 years old when the Dionne Quintuplets were born in 1974.

Mary was 78 years old when she passed away in 1940. She was a member of the Salvation Army.

BETTY GORDON[14]

Betty was born on April 4, 1923. She passed away two days later on April 6th.

GERTRUDE (COULTER) GORDON[15]

Gertrude was born in 1894.

She was 12 years old when Ontario Hydro was established in 1906.

Gertrude was 22 years old when she married Leonard in Kingston, Ontario on January 5, 1916.

She was 29 years old when her daughter, Betty, was born on April 4, 1923. Betty passed away two days later on April 6th.

Gertrude was 40 years old when the Dionne Quintuplets were born in 1934.

She was 55 years old when her mother passed away in 1949.

Gertrude was 57 years old when her father passed away in 1951.

She was 70 years old when she passed away in 1974. Gertrude was Methodist.

JEAN GORDON[16]

Jean was an infant when she passed away. She was Betty Gordon's sister.

LEONARD GORDON[17]

Leonard was born in 1894. He was Scottish.

He was 12 years old when Ontario Hydro was established in 1906.

Leonard was 22 years old when he married Gertrude in Kingston, Ontario on January 5, 1916.

He was 28 years old when his mother passed away in 1922.

Leonard was 29 years old when his daughter, Betty, was born on April 4th, 1923. She passed away on April 6th.

He was 40 years old when the Dionne Quintuplets were born in 1934.

Leonard was 63 years old when his father passed away in 1957.

He was 70 years old when his wife passed away in 1964.

Leonard was 73 years old when he passed away in 1967. He was Methodist.

ANN (ATKINSON) GRAHAM[18]

Ann passed away on November 18, 1815 in Kingston, Frontenac, Upper Canada, British Colonial America.

CATHERINE (GRASS) GRAHAM[19]

Catherine was born in Quebec on December 2, 1783. She was 24 years old when the Atlantic slave trade was abolished in 1808.

Catherine was 26 years old when her daughter, Mary Margaret, was born in 1810.

She was 27 years old when her son, George, was born in 1811.

Catherine was 28 years old when the War of 1812 took place.

She was 29 years old when her daughter, Ann, was born in 1813. Her father passed away the same year.

Catherine was 32 years old when her son, Edward Thomas, was born in 1816. Her sister, Mary, passed away that year.

She was 35 years old when her son, Henry, was born in 1818.

Catherine was 38 years old when her son, John, was born in 1822.

She was 41 years old when her daughter, Jane Harriet, was born in 1825.

Catherine was 63 years old when her husband passed away in 1847.

She was 65 years old when her brother, John, passed away in 1849.

Catherine was 71 years old when her brother, Peter, passed away in 1855.

She was 74 years old when her sister, Eva Margaretha, passed away in 1858.

Catherine was 81 years old when she passed away in Frontenac, Ontario on March 12, 1856.

CHARLES A. GRAHAM[20]

Charles was born in 1850.
He was 64 years old when Canada entered into WWI in 1914.
Charles was 68 years old when he passed away in 1918.

JENNIE GRAHAM[21]

Jennie was the daughter of Charles Graham. She was born in 1883 and passed away a year later in 1884.

JOHN GRAHAM[22]

John was 42 years old when he passed away on January 17, 1853 in Kingston, Frontenac, Canada West, British Colonial America.

JOHN GRAHAM[23]

John was born in 1854.

He was 56 years old when he passed away in 1910.

JOHN GRAHAM[24]

John was born in 1834.

He was 76 years old when he passed away in 1910.

LENA GRAHAM[25]

Lena was born in 1878.

She was five years old when her sister, Jennie, was born in 1883.

Lena was six years old when Jennie passed away in 1884.

She was 40 years old when her father passed away in 1918.

Lena was 69 years old when she passed away in 1947.

ROBERT GRAHAM[26]

R obert passed away on October 26, 1814.

THOMAS GRAHAM[27]

Thomas on September 12, 1787.

He was 21 years old when he married Catherine Grass in Kingston, Ontario on June 22, 1809.

Thomas was 22 years old when his daughter, Mary Margaret, was born in 1810.

He was 23 years old when his son, George, was born in 1811.

Thomas was 25 years old when his daughter, Ann, was born in 1813.

He was 26 years old when his father passed away in 1814.

Thomas was 27 years old when his mother passed away in 1815.

He was 28 years old when his son, Edward Thomas, was born in 1816.

Thomas was 31 years old when his son, Henry, was born in 1818.

He was 35 years old when his son, John, was born in 1822.

Thomas was 35 years old when his daughter, Jane Harriett, was born in 1825.

He was 60 years old when he passed away on October 30, 1847.

WALTER J. GRAHAM[28]

Walter was born in 1895.
He was seven years old when he passed away in 1902.

SANDI GWENDOLYN (MOORE) GRANT[29]

S andi was born on May 10, 1939.
She was 73 years old when she passed away on January 29, 2013.

ALMA MARTHA (SPROULE) GRASS[30]

Alma was born Martha Alma in Kingston, Ontario on December 28, 1879. She was Irish.

She was five years old when the Canadian Pacific Railway was completed in 1885.

Alma was 25 years old when she married Wilbert Leslie Grass in Westbrook, Ontario on October 12, 1905.

She was 27 years old when her daughter, Margaret Ella, was born in 1907.

Alma was 29 years old when her sister, Margaret Maude, passed away in 1909.

She was 33 years old when her son, James Burton, was born in 1913.

Alma was 34 years old when Canada entered into WWI in 1914.

She was 41 years old when her children, Donald Everett and Baby Grass, were born on December 30, 1921. Baby Grass passed away on January 8, 1922.

Alma was 55 years old when her mother passed away in 1935.

She was 57 years old when her father passed away in 1937.

Alma was 77 years old when she passed away in 1957. She was Methodist.

ANNA MARGARETHA (SCHWARTZ) GRASS[31]

Anna was born in Schwaigern, Germany on September 25, 1738. She was christened on the 27th.

She was 21 years old when she married Captain Michael Grass in New York City on May 1, 1760.

Anna was 22 years old when her son, Andreas, was born in 1761.

She was 24 years old when her daughter, Eva Margaretha, was born in 1763.

Anna was 27 years old when her son, J. Michael was born in 1765.

She was 31 years old when her son, Peter, was born in 1770.

Anna was 33 years old when her son, Daniel, was born in 1771.

She was 35 years old when her son, John, was born in 1773.

Anna was 37 years old when her daughter, Anna, was born in 1776.

She was 45 years old when her daughter, Catherine, was born in 1783.

Anna was 73 years old when the War of 1812 took place.

She was 74 years old when her husband passed away in 1813.

Anna was 77 years old when she passed away in 1816.

CATHERINE POLLY (SNOOK) GRASS[32]

Catherine passed away on March 20, 1856.

CHARLOTTE (WARTMAN) GRASS[33]

Charlotte was born in March 1820.

She was 18 years old when her son, Sydney, was born in 1839.

Charlotte was 20 years old when her son, Horace Geoffrey, was born in 1840.

She was 22 years old when her son, John Colburn, was born in 1843.

Charlotte was 26 years old when her daughter, Mary Jane, was born in 1847.

She was 30 years old when her son, Herchmer Wartman, was born in 1850.

Charlotte was 33 years old when her son, Lewis, was born in 1853.

She was 34 years old when her son, William, was born in 1854.

Charlotte was 44 years old when her son, Lewis, passed away in 1864. Lewis was 11 years old.

She was 46 years old when Ontario was founded on July 1, 1867.

Charlotte was 49 years old when she passed away on April 19, 1869.

DANIEL EVERETT EBENEZER GRASS[34]

Daniel was born in Canada West in 1814. He was Dutch.

He was 29 years old when his mother passed away in 1844.

Daniel was 32 years old when his daughter, Hester Amelia, was born in 1847.

He was 34 years old when his son, Michael Henry, was born in 1849.

Daniel was 35 years old when his daughter, Hester, passed away in 1850. Hester was three years old.

He was 36 years old when his son, Peter Maitland, was born in 1852.

Daniel was 40 years old when his father passed away in 1855.

He was 51 years old when Ontario was founded on July 1, 1867.

Daniel was 55 years old when British Columbia joined the confederation in 1871.

He was 69 years old when his brother, Robert Everett, passed away in 1884.

Daniel was 73 years old when his brother, John, passed away in 1889.

He was 79 years old when his brother, Michael Henry, passed away in 1894.

Daniel was 81 years old when his brother, Charles, passed away in 1896.

He was 83 years old when his wife passed away in 1898.

Daniel was 84 years old when his brother, Peter Lewis, passed away in 1899.

He was 88 years old when his sister, Jane Ann, passed away in 1903.

Daniel was 90 years old when Ontario Hydro was established in 1906.

He was 94 years old when he passed away on April 21, 1909. Daniel was Anglican and a farmer.

DONALD EVERETT GRASS[35]

Donald was born in 1921.

He was 13 years old when the Dionne Quintuplets were born in 1934.

Donald was 36 years old when his mother passed away in 1957.

He was 61 years old when the Canada Act was passed in 1982.

Donald was 71 years old when his sister, Margaret Ella, passed away in 1992.

He was 72 years old when he passed away in 1993.

DOUGLAS A. GRASS[36]

Douglas was born in 1952.

He was 17 years old when his brother, Richard, passed away in 1969.

Douglas was 30 years old when the Canada Act was passed in 1982.

He was 41 years old when he passed away in 1993.

ELLA AMELIA (RUNDLE) GRASS[37]

Ella was born in Bloomfield, Ontario on December 26, 1852. She was 14 years old when Ontario was founded on July 1, 1867.

Ella was 18 years old when British Columbia joined the confederation in 1871.

She was 22 years old when she married Peter in Bloomfield, Ontario on November 3, 1875.

Ella was 23 years old when her daughter, Alma May, was born in 1876.

She was 26 years old when her son, Wilbert Leslie, was born in 1879.

Ella was 30 years old when the mining boom in northern Ontario began in 1883.

She was 46 years old when her mother passed away in 1899.

Ella was 53 years old when Ontario Hydro was established in 1906.

She was 69 years old when she passed away on June 5, 1922. Ella was Methodist.

ESTHER (EVERETT) GRASS[38]

Esther was born in 1784.

She was six years old when the first parliament of Upper Canada assembled on September 17, 1791.

Esther was 23 years old when she married Peter on February 9, 1808.

She was 24 years old when her son, Robert Everett, was born on October 12, 1808.

Esther was 24 years old when her son, Peter, was born in 1809.

She was 25 years old when her son, Michael Henry, was born in 1810.

Esther was 27 years old when her son, John, was born in 1812. He passed away that same year.

She was 30 years old when her son, Daniel Everett, was born in 1815.

Esther was 32 years old when her sister, Sarah Ann, passed away in 1817.

She was 33 years old when her son, Peter Lewis, was born in 1817.

Esther was 37 years old when her son, John, was born in 1822.

She was 39 years old when her daughter, Jane Ann, was born in 1823.

Esther was 40 years old when her father passed away in 1825.

She was 42 years old when her son, Charles, was born in 1827.

Esther was 52 years old when her mother passed away in 1837.

She was 59 years old when she passed away in 1844.

HESTER AMELIA GRASS[39]

Hester passed away on July 6, 1850 in Kingston, Frontenac, Canada West, British Colonial America.

IDA W. "BERTIE" (BERTRAND) GRASS[40]

Bertie was born in 1914.

She was 20 years old when the Dionne Quintuplets were born in 1934.

Bertie was 32 years old when her son, Richard, was born in 1946.

She was 38 years old when her son, Douglas, was born in 1952.

Bertie was 55 years old when her son, Richard, passed away in 1969.

She was 68 years old when the Canada Act was passed in 1982.

Bertie was 79 years old when her son, Douglas, passed away in 1993.

She was 82 years old when her husband passed away in 1996.

Bertie was 83 years old when she passed away on February 1, 1997.

J. BURTON "BURT" GRASS[41]

Burt was born in 1813.

He was 21 years old when the Dionne Quintuplets were born in 1934.

Burt was 33 years old when his son, Richard, was born in 1946.

He was 39 years old when his son, Douglas, was born in 1952.

Burt was 44 years old when his mother passed away in 1957.

He was 56 years old when his son, Richard, passed away in 1969.

Burt was 69 years old when the Canada Act was passed in 1982.

He was 79 years old when his sister, Margaret Ella, passed away in 1992.

Burt was 80 years old when his son, Douglas, and brother, Donald Everett, passed away in 1993.

He was 83 years old when he passed away in 1996.

JOHN GRASS[42]

John was born in Collins Bay, Ontario in 1810. He was Dutch.

He was 28 years old when his son, Sydney, was born in 1839.

John was 30 years old when his son, Horace Geoffrey, was born in 1840.

He was 32 years old when his son, John Colburn, was born in 1843.

John was 35 years old when his mother passed away in 1846.

He was 36 years old when his daughter, Mary Jane, was born in 1847.

John was 38 years old when his father passed away in 1849.

He was 40 years old when his son, Herchmer Wartman, was born in 1850.

John was 43 years old when his son, Lewis, was born in 1853.

He was 43 years old when his son, William, was born in 1854.

John was 54 years old when his son, Lewis, passed away in 1864. Lewis was 11 years old.

He was 56 years old when his sister, Hannah Mary, passed away in 1866.

John was 56 years old when his brother, Michael, passed away in 1867.

He was 58 years old when his wife passed away in 1869.

John was 63 years old when his brother, William Lewis, passed away in 1874.

He was 66 years old when his daughter, Mary Jane, passed away in 1877.

John was 67 years old when his sister, Elisabeth, passed away in 1877.

He was 69 years old when his sister, Margaret, passed away in 1880.

John was 72 years old when the mining boom in northern Ontario began in 1883.

He was 73 years old when his brother, Tunis, passed away in 1884.

John was 79 years old when the Women's Suffrage movement began in 1890.

He was 82 years old when he passed away on January 29, 1893 in Collins Bay, Ontario. John is buried in Kingston, Ontario. He was Methodist.

JOHN GRASS SR. [43]

John passed away on January 18, 1849 in Kingston, Frontenac, Canada West. He was a farmer.

LEWIS N. GRASS[44]

Lewis was 10 years and seven months old when he passed away in Kingston, Frontenac, Canada West, on June 11, 1864.

MARGARET ELLA GRASS[45]

Margaret was born in Kingston, Ontario on June 23, 1907. She was 26 years old when the Dionne Quintuplets were born in 1934.

Margaret was 49 years old when her mother passed away in 1957.

She was 74 years old when the Canada Act was passed in 1982.

Margaret was 84 years old when she passed away in 1992. She was Methodist.

CAPTAIN MICHAEL GRASS[46]

(P*lease see footnote for a more detailed biography.)*
Michael passed away on April 25, 1813 in Kingston. He was a Loyalist.

MICHAEL H. GRASS[47]

Michael was born in 1849. He was Dutch.

He was less than a year old when his sister, Hester Amelia, passed away in 1850.

Henry was 17 years old when Ontario was founded on July 1, 1867.

He was 21 years old when British Columbia joined the confederation in 1871.

Henry was 33 years old when the mining boom in northern Ontario began in 1883.

He was 49 years old when his mother passed away in 1898.

Henry was 56 years old when Ontario Hydro was established in 1906.

He was 59 years old when his father passed away in 1909.

Heny was 69 years old when he passed away on September 15, 1918. He was Anglican and a farmer.

NANCY ANN (McGUINN) GRASS[48]

Nancy was born in 1815.

She was 32 years old when her daughter, Hester Amelia, was born in 1847.

Nancy was 34 years old when her son, Michael Henry, was born in 1849.

She was 35 years old when her daughter, Hester Amelia, passed away in 1850. Hester was three years old.

Nancy was 37 years old when her son, Peter Maitland, was born in 1852.

She was 51 years old when Ontario was founded on July 1, 1867.

Nancy was 55 years old when British Columbia joined the confederation in 1871.

She was 83 years old when she passed away on December 11, 1898.

PETER GRASS[49]

Peter passed away on June 27, 1855.

PETER MAITLAND GRASS[50]

Peter was born in Kingston, Frontenac, Canada West in 1852. He was Dutch.

He was 14 years old when Ontario was founded on July 1, 1867.

Peter was 18 years old when British Columbia joined the confederation in 1871.

He was 23 years old when he married Ella Amelia in Bloomfield, Ontario on November 3, 1875.

Peter was 24 years old when his daughter, Alma May, was born in 1876.

He was 27 years old when his son, Wilbert Leslie, was born in 1879.

Peter was 30 years old when the mining boom in northern Ontario began in 1883.

He was 46 years old when his mother passed away in 1898.

Peter was 53 years old when Ontario Hydro was established in 1906.

He was 57 years old when his father passed away in 1909.

Peter was 66 years old when his brother, Michael Henry, passed away in 1918.

He was 70 years old when his wife passed away in 1922.

Peter was 73 years old when he passed away on March 24, 1925. He was Methodist.

RICHARD GRASS[51]

R ichard was born in 1946.
He was 23 years old when he passed away in 1969.

EMMA MAY (RANKIN) GREENWOOD. [52]

Emma was born in Kingston, Ontario on November 15, 1887. Her mother passed away two days later on November 17th.

She was 16 years old when her father passed away in 1903.

Emma was 18 years old when Ontario Hydro was established in 1906.

She was 25 years old when she married Peter Greenwood in Collins Bay, Ontario on April 23, 1913.

Emma was 27 years old when her son, Sidney Hugh John was born in 1915.

She was 46 years old when the Dionne Quintuplets were born in 1934.

Emma was 63 years old when her husband passed away in 1951.

She was 72 years old when she passed away in 1960. Emma was Methodist.

HUGH PAUL GREENWOOD[53]

Hugh was born in 1952.

He was 30 years old when the Canada Act was passed in 1982.

Hugh was 38 years old when he passed away in 1990.

PETER GREENWOOD[54]

Peter was born in Liverpool, England on March 14, 1886.

He was three years old when he immigrated to Canada in 1890.

Peter was 22 years old when his sister, Margaret, passed away in 1908.

He was 27 years old when he married Emma May in Collins Bay, Ontario on April 23, 1913.

Peter was 29 years old when his son, Sidney Hugh John, was born in 1915.

He was 42 years old when his mother passed away in 1929.

Peter was 64 years old when he passed away in 1951.

PHYLLIS CHESTER (LeMAISTRE) GREENWOOD[55]

Phyllis was born in Montreal, Quebec in 1912.

She was 22 years old when the Dionne Quintuplets were born in 1934.

Phyllis was 32 years old when she married Sydney Hugh John in Montreal, Quebec in 1944.

She was 40 years old when her son, Hugh Paul, was born in 1952.

Phyllis was 78 years old when her son passed away in 1990.

She was 82 years old when she passed away in 1994.

SYDNEY HUGH JOHN GREENWOOD[56]

Sydney was born in 1915.

He was 18 years old when the Dionne Quintuplets were born in 1934.

Sydney was 35 years old when his father passed away in 1951.

He was 36 years old when his son, Hugh Paul, was born in 1952.

Sydney was 44 years old when his mother passed away in 1960.

He was 74 years old when his son passed away in 1990.

Sydney was 79 years old when his wife passed away in 1994.

He was 81 years old when he passed away in 1996.

JOHN SAMUEL GRIST[57]

John was born in 1827.

He was 43 years old when British Columbia joined the confederation in 1871.

John was 78 years old when he passed away in 1906. He was Methodist and an architect.

CATHERINE (GROOMS) ASHLEY[58]

Catherine was Methodist.

She passed away on May 9, 1887.

CATHERINE (CRANSTON) GUESS[59]

Catherine was born in 1816.

She was 50 years old when Ontario was founded on July 1, 1867.

Catherine was 54 years old when she passed away in 1870.

EDWARD C. GUESS[60]

Edward was born in the USA in 1803.

He was nine years old when the war of 1812 took place.

Edward was 48 years old when his father passed away in 1851.

He was 59 years old when he passed away on September 14, 1862.

EDWARD FRANCIS GUESS[61]

Edward was born in Kepler, Ontario on June 11, 1844.

He was 15 years old when his brother, James Wesley, passed away in 1859.

Edward was 18 years old when his father passed away in 1862.

He was 22 years old when he married Eleanor Powley in Lennox and Addington, Ontario, on December 25, 1866.

Edward was 22 years old when Ontario was founded on July 1, 1867.

He was 26 years old when his mother passed away in 1870.

Edward was 26 years old when British Columbia joined the confederation in 1871.

He was 30 years old when his daughter, Lillian, was born in 1875.

Edward was 35 years old when his daughter, Elida, and his wife passed away in 1879.

He was 36 years old when he married Mary Jane Wartman in Kingston, Ontario on June 9, 1880.

He was 38 years old when the mining boom in northern Ontario began in 1883.

Edward was 40 years old when his son, Bertram Miller, was born in 1885.

He was 61 years old when Ontario Hydro was established in 1906.

Edward was 75 years old when he passed away on February 1, 1920. He was Irish and Methodist.

JOHN WESLEY GUESS[62]

John was born on August 1, 1831.

He was 28 years old when he passed away on September 3, 1859. John was a Christian.

MARY DAY (WARTMAN) GUESS[63]

Mary was born in 1817. She was Irish.

She was 25 years old when her daughter, Harriet, was born in 1842.

Mary was 27 years old when her son, James Sidney, was born in 1844.

She was 35 years old when her son, Barnabas Secord, was born in 1852.

Mary was 37 years old when her daughter, Calista Ann, was born in 1854.

She was 42 years old when her daughter, Victoria, was born in 1859.

Mary was 46 years old when her daughter, Permilla, was born in 1863. Permilla passed away a year later.

She was 54 years old when British Columbia joined the confederation in 1871.

Mary was 63 years old when she passed away on March 17, 1880. She was Methodist.

SUSANNA (GAINOR) GUESS[64]

Susanna was born in Ireland in 1780.

She was 18 years old when the Young Ireland rebellion of 1798 failed.

Susanna was 23 years old when her son, Edward, was born in 1803.

She was 29 years old when her son, Micajah Purdy, was born in 1809.

Susanna was 33 years old when her son, Francis, was born in 1813.

She was 34 years old when her son, Joel, was born in 1814.

Susanna was 53 years old when her brother, Edward, passed away in 1833.

She was 55 years old when her sister, Nancy, passed away in 1835.

Susanna was 58 years old when her mother passed away in 1838.

She was 67 years old when her father passed away in 1847.

Susanna was 71 years old when her husband passed away in 1851.

She was 82 years old when she passed away on January 3, 1862.

[1] https://www.wikitree.com/genealogy/Gibson-Family-Tree-26085

[2] https://www.wikitree.com/genealogy/McRory-Family-Tree-56

[3] https://www.wikitree.com/genealogy/Bennington-Family-Tree-516

[4] https://www.wikitree.com/genealogy/Gibson-Family-Tree-20967

[5] https://www.wikitree.com/genealogy/Gibson-Family-Tree-26093

[6] https://www.wikitree.com/genealogy/Guess-Family-Tree-826

[7] https://www.wikitree.com/genealogy/Gibson-Family-Tree-26094

[8] https://www.wikitree.com/genealogy/Gibson-Family-Tree-26095

[9] https://www.wikitree.com/genealogy/Gibson-Family-Tree-26097

[10] https://www.wikitree.com/genealogy/Wartman-Family-Tree-82

[11] https://www.wikitree.com/genealogy/Gillespie-Family-Tree-7911

[12] https://www.wikitree.com/genealogy/Glover-Family-Tree-9150

[13] https://www.wikitree.com/genealogy/VanLuven-Family-Tree-53

[14] https://www.wikitree.com/genealogy/Gordon-Family-Tree-18006

[15] https://www.wikitree.com/genealogy/Coulter-Family-Tree-2787

[16] https://www.wikitree.com/genealogy/Gordon-Family-Tree-18507

[17] https://www.wikitree.com/genealogy/Gordon-Family-Tree-13597

[18] https://www.wikitree.com/genealogy/Atkinson-Family-Tree-13177

[19] https://www.wikitree.com/genealogy/Gress-Family-Tree-230

[20] https://www.wikitree.com/genealogy/Graham-Family-Tree-29469

[21] https://www.wikitree.com/genealogy/Graham-Family-Tree-29470

[22] https://www.wikitree.com/genealogy/Graham-Family-Tree-29471

[23] https://www.wikitree.com/genealogy/Graham-Family-Tree-29472

[24] https://www.wikitree.com/genealogy/Graham-Family-Tree-29473

[25] https://www.wikitree.com/genealogy/Graham-Family-Tree-29474

[26] https://cataw.wikitree.com/genealogy/Graham-Family-Tree-29475

[27] https://www.wikitree.com/genealogy/Graham-Family-Tree-29477

[28] https://www.wikitree.com/genealogy/Graham-Family-Tree-29478

[29] https://www.wikitree.com/genealogy/Moore-Family-Tree-77336

[30] https://www.wikitree.com/genealogy/Sproule-Family-Tree-413

[31] https://www.wikitree.com/genealogy/Schwartz-Family-Tree-1507

[32] https://www.wikitree.com/genealogy/Snook-Family-Tree-3025

[33] https://www.wikitree.com/genealogy/Wartman-Family-Tree-83

[34] https://www.wikitree.com/genealogy/Grass-Family-Tree-1004

[35] https://www.wikitree.com/genealogy/Grass-Family-Tree-718

[36] https://www.wikitree.com/genealogy/Grass-Family-Tree-714

[37] https://www.wikitree.com/genealogy/Rundle-Family-Tree-961

[38] https://www.wikitree.com/genealogy/Everett-Family-Tree-1849

[39] https://www.wikitree.com/genealogy/Grass-Family-Tree-1005

[40] https://www.wikitree.com/genealogy/Bertrand-Family-Tree-1701

[41] https://www.wikitree.com/genealogy/Grass-Family-Tree-715

[42] https://www.wikitree.com/genealogy/Gress-Family-Tree-236

[43] https://www.wikitree.com/genealogy/Grass-Family-Tree-434

[44] https://www.wikitree.com/genealogy/Grass-Family-Tree-1007

[45] https://www.wikitree.com/genealogy/Grass-Family-Tree-716

[46] https://www.wikitree.com/genealogy/Grass-Family-Tree-217

[47] https://www.wikitree.com/genealogy/Grass-Family-Tree-1008

[48] https://www.wikitree.com/genealogy/McQuinn-Family-Tree-602

[49] https://www.wikitree.com/genealogy/Gress-Family-Tree-227

[50] https://www.wikitree.com/genealogy/Grass-Family-Tree-1009

[51] https://www.wikitree.com/genealogy/Grass-Family-Tree-713

[52] https://www.wikitree.com/genealogy/Rankin-Family-Tree-4975

[53] https://www.wikitree.com/genealogy/Greenwood-Family-Tree-3585

[54] https://www.wikitree.com/genealogy/Greenwood-Family-Tree-3580

[55] https://www.wikitree.com/genealogy/LeMaistre-Family-Tree-84

[56] https://www.wikitree.com/angealogy/Greenwood-Family-Tree-5203

[57] https://www.wikitree.com/genealogy/Grist-Family-Tree-702

[58] https://www.wikitree.com/genealogy/Grooms-Family-Tree-849

[59] https://www.wikitree.com/genealogy/Cranston-Family-Tree-974

[60] https://www.wikitree.com/genealogy/Guess-Family-Tree-827

[61] https://www.wikitree.com/genealogy/Guess-Family-Tree-828

[62] https://www.wikitree.com/genealogy/Guess-Family-Tree-829

[63] https://www.wikitree.com/genealogy/Day-Family-Tree-14284

[64] https://www.wikitree.com/genealogy/Gainor-Family-Tree-56

Don't miss out!

Visit the website below and you can sign up to receive emails whenever Angeline Gallant publishes a new book. There's no charge and no obligation.

https://books2read.com/r/B-A-QGSI-PJTCC

Connecting independent readers to independent writers.

Also by Angeline Gallant

Calling Her Heart
Whisper of the Heart
No Turning Back
Forsake Me Not
Hear My Cry
Calling Her Heart Boxed Set Volumes 1-4

FORGET ME NOT
Victoria, Ontario's Babies 1894 - 1895

Keeper Of Secrets
A Lady's Secret

Midnight's Awakening
Heart of the Storm
Walking Through The Storm
Midnight's Awakening boxed set volumes 1-3

Secrets of the Underworld
Deklan's Dragons
Secrets of the Underworld Volumes 1 & 2

Tell My Story Collection
Tell My Story: England 1852

The Grave Whisperer
Wedding Bells in Kingston, Ontario, Canada 1923
St. Paul's Anglican Churchyard Kingston, Ontario, Canada A-B
St. Paul's Anglican Churchyard, Kingston, Ontario, Canada C - D
St. Paul's Anglican Churchyard, Kingston, Ontario, Canada G - H
St. Paul's Anglican Churchyard, Kingston, Ontario, Canada J - N
St. Paul's Anglican Churchyard, Kingston, Ontario, Canada O - R
St. Paul's Anglican Churchyard, Kingston, Ontario, Canada S - T
St. Paul's Anglican Churchyard, Kingston, Ontario T - Z
Small Graveyards & Burial Grounds: Kingston, Ontario, Canada
Cataraqui United Church Cemetery 1
Cataraqui United Church Cemetery 2
Cataraqui United Church Cemetary 3
Cataraqui United Church Cemetery 4
Cataraqui United Church Cemetery 5

The Wolf Whisperer Series
The Cry of the Wolf
Captured Heart

Journey of the Heart
Fate's Legacy
Wolf Whisperer volumes 1 & 2
Endless White
The Wolf Whisperer Volumes 1-4

Standalone
Winds of Change vol 1-3